It's All Your Fault

A Survivor's Guide to Narcissism

By

Jennifer M. Baldwin

Text copyright 2016 Jennifer M. Baldwin

All Rights Reserved

This book is dedicated to everyone who is healing from an abusive relationship.

To those of you who have stuck by us and helped glue the broken parts back together, we thank you.

Table of Contents

Introduction

I'm going to make a pretty bold assumption right now. You saw the title of this book and something in you grew curious. You or someone you know is in a relationship with a malignant narcissist. Or maybe you don't know if you are, but you know something isn't quite right in your relationship. And you don't know what to do.

This book is here to help. You'll learn what a narcissist is and their tactics. You'll learn why you became a target and how to stop being a victim. You'll learn ways to heal and move on and maybe even help someone else in the same situation.

I'll introduce you to several people: Dan, Michelle, and Ann. They don't represent any one person. They are each an amalgam of other people I've interviewed in their particular positions. I want to thank everyone who shared their stories with me. You helped me craft the three main characters you'll meet.

Since I've introduced the book and characters, let me introduce myself. I'm Jen. I'm a 38 year old stay at home mom from Philadelphia. I moved out to southwest Missouri with my narcissist in 2002. I picked up and left a job I had for five years. I left my friends, my family, and everything I knew and loved to move to a place where I knew no one. There was no phone in the house when we moved in. He went on the road, truck driving, leaving me completely isolated for three months. I had nothing but him.

That was the beginning of my time in Hell. Ten years later, he had finally grown tired of me and tossed me out. In that ten years so much happened. I look back at it like living with a disease. At first you don't know what's wrong, you just know it's not normal to have a bruise or cough that long. Your symptoms worsen over time, but you've gotten so used to the minor ones you don't notice them anymore. They've become a way of life. Others around you will say things like, "Maybe you should get that checked out. That's not normal." But it's your life and you're happy and everything's fine. Thats what you tell yourself every morning in the mirror. The years of crying and no sleep have started showing on your face.

Then one day a symptom shows up that you can't ignore. For me, it was getting kicked out. I had served my purpose. He used me up. He had already been working and grooming his next victim, my replacement. I was the proverbial cheese; I stood alone.

What was his ultimate checkmate turned out to be my turning point for growth and survival. It's been four years now. I have a loving, amazing, supportive husband. He is an incredible father to our toddler son and stepfather to my teen daughter. He is a shining example of why it didn't work out with my narc. He has been with me through so many horrible, ugly moments while dealing with my ex. At any point he could have left, but he didn't. Much of my strength came from him. I thank the Universe every day for him.

This book came out of a need to share my story and the stories of others. I knew there were other people in the same type of situation. I knew if I had found a book I would have been able to save myself a lot of pain, frustration, and humiliation. This is the book I needed. If this is the book you need, I'm glad I wrote it. I use male pronouns throughout this book. I am aware there are female narcissists.

I hope this helps you.

Preface

We just got done watching 10 Cloverfield Lane. If you haven't seen it, go watch it. I'll wait. Ok, did you watch it? Pretty good, right? Yeah, I dug it. But, the more I watched, the more I realized what this movie was actually about. If you didn't watch it, be aware I'm going to unload spoilers all over the place. More like I'm going to run down the whole story so this is your final warning. If you haven't seen the movie but, you want to then stop reading now!

You have this young lady, Michelle, who runs away from the hard times. It's her coping device, dysfunctional as it may be, but it's worked for her so far. As she's once again running from her problems she's in a car accident. Waking up, she discovers an iv of fluids hooked into her arm and a knee brace chained to the wall. This is where I started to notice a theme.

In walks Howard, a large, older male, who is definitely in control. Howard shows no compassion or empathy. He doesn't try to comfort Michelle. In fact, he seems quite content in the fact she is feared him and the situation she's in. He lets her know that at every opportunity he can. He has no problem telling her that he saved her life and how she should be grateful for everything he has done for her. Under no circumstance should she question anything Howard tells her. about what's going on outside of his little bunker below the farmhouse. If he says the air is toxic and will kill you then you better believe it. If he tells you all your friends and family are dead, then no one is looking for you. There's no point in trying to escape.

In this post apocalyptic survival bunker there is an injured younger male. When Michelle asks how he got his injury, a busted arm in a sling, Howard appears. He explains Emmett was the cause of his own injuries by stumbling around.

From the start Howard gave me the chills, like the hints of a nightmare you can't remember all the pieces to. I couldn't quite figure out why this movie was making me so uncomfortable. My skin crawled and my stomach turned. This was not your standard horror movie, no blood or gore, no killers with machetes or chain saws. This felt personal. And then I got it.

This was the story of domestic abuse and the courage to escape and survive. This was a survival story. Howard is a bully and he uses the fact that he saved Michelle to his advantage. Now isolated from the world outside the bunker the only information she has Howard gave her. He tried to garner sympathy by telling a story of his daughter and wife leaving him. You have to feel sorry for him, he only tried to do the best he could and no one appreciated him and his hard work. When Michelle doesn't show Howard gratitude he flies into a rage.

Using her skills as a clothing designer, Michelle makes a Biohazard suit. She summons up her courage and escapes. It wasn't easy. Howard discovered her plans and fought and chased. But she made it out. And this is where the real survival story starts as it does with many survivors of domestic violence.

So many times abuse victims hear they will never survive outside of the relationship. You're not smart enough, pretty enough, you don't have any money. The only way you can live is with me. No one else will take you. Michelle learns there are dangers out in the world and Howard wasn't as crazy as he sounded. Michelle digs down deep and summons courage greater than that of any superhero. As she drives away, a voice comes over the radio that Howard said had no signal. There are survivors and they need help in Houston. Staring at the road signs, Michelle decides to stop running away from danger and to help others.

Am I looking into this too much? Maybe. But this was the message I got from this movie. Here's a girl who finds herself in an abusive relationship. And yes, I mean finds. Too many times victims wake up and realize this has been going on all along but they couldn't see it. And despite the bullying and terror, in the face of certain death, she escapes. The experience has changed her. Instead of running away, she decides to help others become survivors rather than victims.

I've had people ask me what the point of my writing is. Why do I blog? What do I hope to achieve through this? I want to be like Michelle and help people realize the strength that lies within them. Michelle had a greatness inside her. Many times, our own greatness doesn't show up until an emergency presents itself. How many times have you said to yourself, "I didn't know I had it in me." Your greatness came through for you. You need that greatness to reveal itself as if your life depends on it. Because it does. Through your greatness, others may have a better chance of seeing their potential. Because you didn't give up, other survivors will be able to continue to make the world a better place.

If you're in an abusive relationship, please call this number 1-800-799-7233. That is the domestic abuse hotline. You deserve to live in peace and without fear and bruises.

Chapter 1

What is a narcissist?

Narcissist personality disorder is an inflated sense of self importance. There is no cure, but treatment can help. It is more common in males. It's characterized by an excessive need for admiration. There is a general disregard for others' feelings. Narcissists have an inability to handle criticism, and a sense of entitlement. Narcissists tend to be cold, calculating, callous, and unemotional.

That's the textbook definition. In reality, it's much more complicated than that. We all can think of people that we've known throughout our lives that fit that description. This is so much more than the cheerleaders in high school that would flip out if their hair wasn't perfect. It's bigger than your high school teacher who thought he was God's gift of teaching. It's the partner that starts the relationship by putting you on a pedestal. He ends it by kicking you out and replacing you with another willing victim. Between points A and B is mental, verbal, and emotional abuse.

Nothing is his fault. He will always deny that his actions cause you any harm. It won't matter how much time you spend laying out his actions and words and how they hurt you. It doesn't hurt him so it doesn't matter.

Everything is always all about him. An artist in his own right the narc invents a fairy tale land where he is king. As long as his kingdom is perfect from the outside to people who don't live there everything is great. It doesn't matter that the kingdom is actually devoid of all life and starting to crumble in on itself. On the surface, it's perfect. And as long as he can control the picture others sees everything is okay. This is why he lies. He tells you these lies to control your behavior and not your thinking. He tells these lies making them so absurd and grandiose waiting for you to call him out on it. He will cover you in emotional vomit about how you never trust him (projection). You always do this to him (he's the victim). It's not like he was serious anyway; he was just joking (minimization).

My Way or the Highway

There is only one way to do something and it's his way. Lets take the house keeping for example. Dan had a certain way he loads the dishwasher. If Michelle didn't load the dishwasher his way, then Dan punished her. His choice of punishment was taunts, name calling, and general shaming. This was a behavior not just saved for the family behind closed doors; it was also done in front of company. Dan thought this made him look like the king of the castle. Michelle felt humiliated and disappointed in herself. Yet again, she couldn't make Dan happy despite her best efforts. This was another deserved shaming. She disappointed him, again. That's all she ever seemed to be able to do right was disappointing him.

This is exactly the reaction the narc is going for. This is part of the devalue stage. He is taking away your power and strength and self worth. The less you believe you're worth, the more he can pile on you and the more you will take.

Never wrong

It doesn't matter what the subject is, he's an expert. He knows all and don't you dare contradict him. Even if you can prove to him you're right, you're wrong. The fact is he knows he's wrong. He may not know it to start, but when you say, "You know I don't think it's ABC, I think it's xyz." He'll recognize your answer is right but since he can never be wrong he will stick to his guns. He will blame you for making him look bad.

Watching Mrs. Doubtfire, Dan remarked he didn't believe Robin Williams was the old woman. He said it had to be some old, washed up actress. This confused Michelle. They had watched a documentary about movie makeup featuring Mrs. Doubtfire. When Michelle brought that up, Dan immediately asked why she was trying to start a fight. A fight was the last thing Michelle wanted. So instead of pushing the issue, she just dropped it and sat in silence for the rest of the film. Dan saw this as a win. He got to be right and project his insecurities on Michelle. Even better for him, he put her in her place. She learned who's boss and who was in control.

Perfect on the Outside

Narcissists would rather impress strangers than their own families. The narc values the opinions of strangers and the general public over those closest to him. Image is everything. The fact that he's negligent and abusive behind closed doors means nothing to him. He seems to be the perfect husband or father outside of the home. To the outside world he is so caring and involved. He's the first one at parent teacher conferences. He always brags about how smart and talented his kids are. All week at the office, he talks about how this weekend they're all going to the park or zoo. It doesn't matter that all he does is tell people he goes to the parent teacher conference. He is actually home playing video games. He tells everyone how talented his daughter is but complains about the art supplies. He talks about trips to the park or zoo all week, but Saturday morning comes around and now his back hurts. He's worked hard all week and he deserves some time for himself. He never had any intention of going to the zoo, but it made him look like super dad to his co-workers. that was the end goal.

Chapter 2

Tactics

Narcissists have an ample toolbag of methods they dig into on a regular basis. these behaviors range from lying to ignoring you to shaming you. Each strategy has one goal, control. He's controlling you, how others see you, and how much contact you have with your friends and family. He is all about control.

Hugging the Cold Shoulder

This is a favorite scheme of narcissists - the silent treatment. If you bring up something they don't want to discuss, like their abuse, they will stop talking to you. Think teenage girl with her headphones on. Yeah, it's that immature. He'll talk about you, over you, and around you, but he won't address you. He does this to get you to ask what's wrong. He'll then blame you for trying to start drama. Weird how that works.

Poor Poor Pitiful Me

This takes advantage of your natural inclination to help people. To get attention, they will fake illnesses and injuries. He will lie about crimes against him, and talk about crazy exes that did him wrong. The whole point of this plan is to make you feel sorry for him and strengthen the bond between you both. This ploy helps make them seem capable of real emotions.

Them vs you

Watch for triangulation, pitting you against his mom, ex, kids, or friends. The definition of triangulation is: one individual abusing another person using someone else. He will tell you Mary said XYZ about you then tell Mary you said XYZ about her. Then, he will sit back and watch the fire he started burning while claiming no responsibility for any of it. This is to get you to try and defend yourself because the more you try to defend yourself the crazier you look.

Triangulation is communication and behaviors that involve three or more people. It is identified by spying, lying, and abuse. You might remember a time you bought the stories. You believed him about discrediting others.

There are three roles in triangulation.

The Persecutor

This is the starring role for your narcopath. This role draws high conflict personalities. The irony is the persecutor completely believes he is the victim. Narcissists do not admit or take responsibility for their actions. It's all about setting the blame on you. He makes you feel guilty, and gets others to believe you're the bad guy. He will need to recruit allies. The narcissist is powerless. He needs to rally people as reinforcements to completely discredit you.

Many people believe the narcissist's lies. Why would someone say something unless it was true?! If you're lucky, someone the narc goes to will come to you for the truth instead of believing him. not all who get invited into the flying monkey circus join. They may still offer sympathy to the provoker but they won't join in on his reindeer games.

The Rescuer

Triangulation includes a fictitious character, a real person, or a fabricated statement. Narcissists often use third person statements when trying to discredit you.

Dan was talking to Michelle during one of his attempts to cause trauma and drama. "I was speaking with Will. He and Ann both agree that you need to see a doctor for your mood swings. They don't like hanging out with us much because you're so unpredictable. He said You kind of scare them. They also said they can tell how it's affecting our relationship."

In this case, Will and Ann are real people who think Dan is a good person and their friend. The problem is we don't know if they actually said any of that or just offered a sympathetic ear. Either way, Dan has recruited flying monkeys. Unless Michelle goes to Will or Ann and asks if they said any of that then she won't know the truth. Just the truth portrayed to her by Dan. And that's how he likes it. Now Michelle feels even more alone and isolated. People she thought were her friends are talking about her. She's also thinking maybe she should go to a doctor and that everyone is right. She's crazy. Dan has succeeded in causing turmoil.

What Will and Ann don't realize is that they are also victims of Dan's abuse. Trust me, Dan will have no problem lashing out at either one of them the minute they don't do what he wants. He is lying to them and using them. He has no problem using them as speed bumps if they try throwing him under the bus to serve his purpose. These people are objects and when their usefulness is complete he discards them. That doesn't stop the narc from bringing them back into the three ring circus of mayhem. At that point it's up to them if they join again.

The Persecuted

Narcissists are experts at playing out reactions. They flip the script to make people look at you like you're the crazy one. The more upset you get and the more you try to defend yourself the guiltier you look. It will only get worse. The more you try to prove your sanity and innocence, and to expose the narc the more you play into what he wants. This gives the narc more power and strengthens his grip on your image and reputation with others. Your best defense is to think of yourself as a rock: no contact, no reaction, no emotion.

I'll Get You, My Pretty

Beware his enablers aka flying monkeys. These are people who help the narc in his abuse. They will spy on the victim and spread gossip. They will also help the narcissist look like the victim. They are his own little fan club. They know he's abusive and still keep a friendship with him. They are toxic. Especially treacherous and heartbreaking is when they masquerade as your friends. They think they'll never fall victim to the ringleader's abuse. These clowns are not immune to the narcopath's wrath. Flying monkeys are scapegoats. They will learn this if they step out of line.

It's Not That Bad

I won't lie; this is my absolute most hated technique. This is an invalidation of your emotions and makes the statement, "You don't matter. You don't count. You and your feelings are a joke!" This is minimization. It's characterized by telling you to calm down, and they didn't mean what they said. It was just a joke. This type of behavior has another message if you choose to hear it: "Don't believe anything I say. I'm lying all the time and you can't trust anything I say."

Michelle was late coming home from work one night. One of the parents at the daycare got a flat tire on the way. No big deal; it happens every now and then. As she walked in the door, Dan started grilling her about where she' been and who she's been with. While she's explaining, Dan cuts her off, stating, "You were screwing one of the dads." He said it like he was ordering a burger and fries. This hits Michelle hard; she has never cheated on Dan or given him reason to think she has. She explained the child and his parents' names, where the mom worked, where she broke down. All this to assure Dan there was no hanky panky going on. Finally, after getting the reaction he was looking for, Dan chimed in. "I was just kidding. I was just joking. Can't you take a joke?" Michelle then had to deal with her feelings and the confusion from the whole episode. Dan had succeeded in causing chaos for Michelle.

I call this tactic the cover your ass method. In my experience, the narcopath will say something and wait to gauge your reaction. He will deploy this scheme when he sees you're upset. That's when he says you misunderstood what he meant. Not what he said, just the meaning behind the words. He'll blame you for being too sensitive. This ploy allows for his inappropriate behavior while blaming you for your offense. You're supposed to just get over it. Meaning sit down and shut up. Let me say and do anything and everything I want with no repercussions because you don't matter. "I was just kidding." No, you weren't. You were dead serious and you don't want to own up to it.

Poking the Tiger

Another favorite method for the narcissist is to provoke the target. He does this with sarcasm, jokes, minimization, and patronization. The target tries to laugh it off and remain calm, but after a while can only take so much and explodes. The provoker will act shocked and will wonder what could have made the victim react in such a manner. Shaming the victim for reacting is the next step in this process. This results in the victim feeling guilty and apologizing for losing their temper. This ensures the narc will be able to provoke more next time and the target will be less likely to defend herself.

Dan walked into the living room and found Michelle studying for an upcoming test. Michelle was competitive and liked having the highest grades in her class. She saw this as an opportunity to improve their financial status. Succeeding in this class was crucial to her planning for the future. Dan started asking Michelle questions about the bank balance, her schedule, and what was dinner. Each question distracted her and forced her to start over again. Michelle asked him to leave her alone so she could study. His response was to turn on a video game and play it as loud as he could without the neighbors calling the cops (again). After trying to concentrate, Michelle started packing her books to go to the library. "Where are you going? What's wrong? Why are you mad?" he yelled out the door as she walked down the steps. "Away from you!" she yelled back over her shoulder. Dan had evidence now that she was the aggressor; everyone in the apartment complex heard her yell at him. After all, he was just concerned about her bad mood and where she was going.

Waves of chaos

Everyone has fights and down times and rough spots. Healthy individuals get over those. Narcs bring chaos and leave a wake of destruction. Look for failing friendships, jealousies, and mood swings. Look to see who is sitting back, calm and collected, cool as a cucumber pickling in his own self entitlement. He is Nero fiddling as Rome burns around him. The best way to fight this is to start comparing notes. If you hear Mary is saying ABC to you then go to Mary and ask her in the least confrontational way possible. Tell Mary you heard from the narc she was saying ABC about you. Once you two start putting the pieces together, you'll both find out you've been pawns. It's a sick game neither of you could win. At this point you can both choose to confront the narc with your findings. Prepare for the narc to deflect and project. Remember nothing is his fault. He's the victim and you're mean because you didn't believe him. The fact that he lied is irrelevant.

Gaslighting

This makes you question your memory. It's a form of brainwashing that makes you think you're crazy. The narcissist will deny facts, events, and what was or wasn't said. It leaves you anxious, confused, and distrusting of your own self. Narcissists are pathological liars, so this tactic is easy for them to pull this off. The target will always second guess every little detail of every conversation and event. Making simple decisions is no longer simple. Making excuses for his behavior becomes normal. Nothing you do is right. When you bring up his past misdeeds, confront him with the truth, or expose him as a fraud he will retaliate. You're the crazy one. You never remember anything right. He will accuse you of being dramatic and having an over active imagination. You are the cause of all the problems and everyone else thinks so too. Even after going over the facts he will deny everything and make up a whole new story. Your inability to recall the events is just further proof that you need medication. You're the sick one. Narcissists actually believe their own lies and stories. to them, its not lying; it is the truth as they see it.

Projection
　　　　Narcissists project because they can't and won't take responsibility for their actions.

Projection ensures two things:

1) Punishment for questioning the image the narc is portraying, and

2) You are the cause of the injustices in his life.

The narc sees you as a mirror, reflecting back all those pesky flaws right in their own eyes. They can't handle who they are so they throw it all at you to own. It's a game of hot potato and they always want to win. You can guarantee everything they say you are and what you do is his acknowledgement of his own issues. When you understand all this, you can see that the narcissist speaks to a mirror.

The best advice I can give is don't listen. This is a dangerous game he is playing. This is where his voice can become your inner voice. It is causing you to doubt yourself, and changing your self image. Depression is a real symptom and an effect of this kind of abuse. It's exhausting trying to shield yourself from this kind of negativity 24/7.

Projection is all about accusing you of the behaviors they engage in. In a projection phase, the narcissist will start many of his sentences with You. "You always... You never... You don't..." Whatever he is saying about you, that's how he sees himself. We all have that one friend who can't figure out why her partner is accusing her of cheating. She's a stay at home mom chasing toddlers all day. The most adventurous trips are to Walmart with the kids. And yet he swears she's cheating. What's the first thing that goes through your mind when you hear this? He's cheating and blaming her. It's easier for him to blame her for his bad behavior. Remember, nothing is his fault anyway.

Deflection

When confronted with the truth the narcissist will change the subject. They do this to avoid responsibility. Dan had been running to Michelle's friend, Ann, telling her that Michelle had said abc about her. He was also telling Michelle that Ann was saying ABC about her. Michelle and Ann worked together. It didn't take long for them to figure out Dan was running a game on both of them just to see them fight. Remember, drama is narc crack. Michelle and Ann decided to confront Dan with their findings. Instead of realizing the jig is up and admitting what he did, Dan started accusing them of ganging up on him. "You always do this. You never trust me. Why did you have to talk to her? You're just looking for a fight."

Chapter 3

Cycle of Abuse
Assess

What do you have that they want? Remember, it's all about them. They will see what you have to offer that they can take advantage of. It could be you're a caring ear, you have money, or you represent everything they want and want to be. Whatever it is, they will try to use you up and leave you a dry hollow husk of your former self. At no point will they think about what they can do for you just to be nice. It is always with the end result of what can they get out of it.

Dan is excellent at landscaping, particularly lawn mowing. Ann is busy with her own business so she asks Dan if he would help her out. Ann is willing to pay, but Dan is never satisfied with just that. He has her pay him, pay for the gas for the mower, take him to dinner, and watch his daughter. The same situation happens if she has a problem with her car.

There will always be an imbalance; your debt to him never gets any lighter. He sees that you need something and he wants something you have. He will take full advantage of you. After all, if it weren't for him this problem wouldn't get solved.

Idolization

He will praise, worship, and buy gifts so you feel obliged to him and will do what he says and wants. This is also known as love bombing.

Love bombing is so called because of the constant positive attention from the Narcopath. Love bombing is effective, as it quickly moves the relationship forward. This happens in many different ways: texting, comments on your social media, calls and messages. He might shower you with gifts and fancy dinners, and compliment you all the time. You might spend 10 hours talking on a telephone conversation.

This is brainwashing in its simplest form. The message you're meant to receive is:

He likes me. We have so much in common, I've never met anyone that is so much like me. It feels like I've known him all my life.

At first you're going to be in heaven. I mean, who doesn't love being in love. The start of a relationship just feels wonderful. The clouds are fluffier, birds sing a little sweeter, and your job doesn't suck so much.

You'll leave each other little love notes, and send sweet good morning and good night texts. It is like something from a Nicholas Sparks novel. That's because it is like that, it's fiction, not real at all.

He has already assessed you and seen what he has to gain by entering a relationship with you. Now he's mirroring you and giving you what you want to hear and feel. This is all about control. He is sucking up all your free time to have your full and complete attention. He's now the center of your universe. And that's how he likes it and wants it and will do whatever it takes to keep it that way.

This is a key tool for a narcopath. There are specific reasons this phase takes place.
It happens so fast you don't get a chance to think about what's happening. This is a prime example of a head over feet, head spinning, whirlwind romance. It isolates you from friends and family by keeping you all to himself. After all, why wouldn't you want to spend all your waking hours with someone who loves you so much?

Michelle and Dan had been dating for two and a half months. Her parents didn't like him and her friends had all stopped talking to her. But she was happier than she had been in a long time. Because Dan was an over the road truck driver, he would often stay at Michelle's apartment when he was in town. After four months of dating Dan moved into the apartment. He also started volunteering at the community center Michelle worked at. When Michelle got a part time job at the mall, Dan quit driving and started working at the same store in the mall. He even requested to have the same shifts so they could be together even more. At six months into the relationship, Dan proposed. Everyone in Michelle's life was trying to tell her this was moving all too fast, but she didn't listen. He was perfect, misunderstood, and lonely. He was a broken soul just crying out for love and healing. In her eyes, he was everything he wanted her to see. He had her hooked.

Be careful who sweeps you off your feet. They may not always catch you when you fall.

Devalue

It's time to play the shame and blame game. Now with more name calling and nit picking. This is the biggest part of the narc pie. This is the part of the program when he starts chipping away at your self esteem and self worth. You'll start doubting your memory, your friends and family, and yourself. He will single you out, put you in the spotlight, and shove you in a closet to suit his needs. Your accomplishments are his. You are nothing. Your kids are his kids when they are being good and well behaved. Once they disobey him or don't pull an A in school you have failed as a mother. Nothing you do or say will be good enough or right. You'll start to notice others treat you differently. This is because the narc is talking about you to them and not in the most flattering ways.

Michelle was walking around downtown and decided to surprise her husband at his job. When she got there Dan had already left to meet her at the bank. That's what his co-workers told her. Dan's co-workers noticed Michelle's confusion. They asked if it was from the medication. What medication? Michelle discovered Dan told his co-workers she had been in the hospital for stress. That's why he was taking so much time off to help take care of her. Embarrassed, Michelle excused herself to go meet her husband at the bank. She could hear the whispers as she left. What a good husband he was to deal with that. Yeah. Great.

Discard

He's used you up. There's no reward for him to keep you around anymore, so to the curb you go so he can move on to the next willing participant. This is a blessing and a curse. You'll think this is the worst day in your life. He's doing you a favor. You may notice it doesn't take him long to have a new partner. He was working on love bombing her before you got to this phase.

Michelle and Dan had just moved to a new house. One week after moving in, Michelle came home from work and found her clothes in trash bags on the bed. Someone else's clothes were in the closet. That's a hell of a hint.

Hoovering

Even after tossing you out like yesterday's kitty litter, he doesn't want you moving on. He will try to suck you back in with pleas of forgiveness and promises of change. None are sincere. He just wants to keep you from healing. He may use you in his new relationship as proof of his crazy ex.

Shortly after Dan kicked her out, Michelle started looking for a place for her and her daughter to live. During the search for an affordable place, they stayed at Ann's house. For two weeks, Dan left messages ranging in tone from apologizing to threatening. He asked if they had a place to stay because if not they could stay in the back room of the house he just kicked them out. The same house he was now living in with his new girlfriend and her kids. Dan wanted to have his cake and eat it too. Because Michelle didn't have a permanent address, Dan reported her to the Division of Children's Services for neglect. At several points he threatened to take their daughter. He "never kicked her out, just you, so that's kidnapping."

Even after Michelle found a place to stay and had a new love interest, Dan continued his harassment. He left voice mail messages threatening to drive his truck through the house. He texted messages saying he's going to set the house on fire. He made calls to animal control to have them arrested for animal cruelty because their cat ran away.

With all this going on he invited Michelle and Jack to dinner. He went so far to invite them over to his house to celebrate his stepdaughter's birthday. It was his weekend with his daughter so she was there visiting during the party. When Dan and Michelle's daughter wanted to go home Dan threw a tantrum. Michelle must have said something to their daughter just to ruin the party. This kind of back and forth behavior went on for four years.

Michelle finally had to realize what he was doing. She went to a no contact rule unless through text plan so she could keep records of all conversations. When their daughter turned thirteen, Michelle gave her the option of when she would visit her dad. Since there were no lawyers or courts involved in their split up, she was within her rights to do so. Things are much more relaxed and calm for Michelle, and her daughter, and Jack. Michelle saw the game Dan was playing and she changed the rules of engagement. Now she has the power. Now she's in control.

Chapter 4

Is Your Relationship Abusive?

Is this what a healthy relationship looks like?

It's an odd thing when you see memes and posts on social media related to domestic abuse if you've been in a relationship with a narcissist. It's even stranger if you're an Empath no longer in that relationship. You read and acknowledge the trigger warnings, but it doesn't help. You start to relive arguments and fights and screaming matches. You start to feel the shame and guilt that never should have been yours to start with. And you get that nagging voice in your head that says, "He never hit you so it's not abuse. You're not a victim."

But you are. And you're a survivor. You're not a loser, pathetic, weak, or stupid. You are a special soul; you are an Empath. Your energy is attractive to narcissists. They play everyone, but you were special because you played back. Like a sick game of tennis this goes back and forth. He needs someone to listen to him, believe him, care about him. You need to fix the broken people in the world. And that's how the cycle begins.

In the beginning everything is beautiful. You're both in love. He takes you out and buys you things. Then, he starts opening up to you about his past and all the pain he's endured. And like a good little sponge you sit there and listen and absorb it all. His mom neglected him, his dad abused him, his mom neglected him, his sisters tortured him. And you listen. You feel sorry for this poor, broken, wounded soul. You can fix him; you can heal the pain.

But you can't. You really can't. When you try that's when you'll see a different side. When you point out a difference in a story he's told repeatedly he'll say you're wrong. You didn't hear it right. Your memory is going; you've always had a bad memory anyway. You'll go to call your sister to ask if she noticed that you had a bad memory growing up. But then you'll remember you haven't spoken to her in a few months. Or any friends. You used to see your parents every day and that's dropped to once a week, for only an hour at best. Something has changed. You are changing.

You used to be bright, and funny, and energetic. You don't watch certain movies or tv shows anymore because he thinks they're stupid. Why would you want to watch this crap? You don't read nearly as much as you did. There are books everywhere! Are they more important than me? You don't talk much anymore because nothing you say is right. Now you slump, and cry, and barely talk to anyone. Friday Karaoke and Saturday at the bar don't happen anymore. You look in the mirror, but you're not sure who it is looking back. What's changed?

You now have someone who is candy coated poison living with you. That candy coating drew you in. You've become an ant on a lollipop that got stuck without even realizing it. Is this what a healthy relationship looks like? Ridicule, and snide remarks. Lies set up to make you look stupid. He saves the poison for private, at home moments. You didn't load the dishes right again; how many times do I have to show you how to do this? Are you really going to wear that out; you look like a potato? Why are you taking that class, you never stick with anything anyway. Slowly but surely his voice becomes the one you hear when you're alone. His voice becomes your voice. All those horrible, nasty opinions of his become your reality.

On the outside, he shows that candy off like it's going out of style. You hear how lucky you are and you better marry this one before he gets away. You start thinking maybe it's you. Maybe you're the crazy one. It's not that bad is it? After all, he doesn't hit you. Just the doors and walls. And he broke the picture frames. And the coffee table. But it's ok. Maybe it is just me. It's normal to be afraid to come home. It's normal to get twenty texts in an hour asking where you are, when are you coming home, who are you with. It's normal getting voice mails yelling about you not picking up the phone. It doesn't matter if you're at work and could lose your job if you did. He's the priority. Your job doesn't matter. He makes way more money than you anyway. And you better be damn glad he does because he supports your dumb, lazy self. And don't you forget it. But he loves you.

    You don't have to live like this. You deserve better. You can find someone to love you despite what he has said. You're not crazy, he is. Before you think you're depressed make sure you're not surrounded by assholes. Or just one in particular because typically he'll have you isolated. That way you have to depend on him. Which is quite amusing because he's the one that needs you even though he has you convinced you need him. You're his battery. It's through you that he has power. Without you he is nothing. Without you, he has no one to listen to his poor pitiful me stories or believe his lies.

You are a powerful force in this world. You see people and feel their pain and joy like no other creature. There will always be people who will try to steal your sunshine. You're better than that. You are stardust. Don't let them steal your sparkle. And you learn the signs of a narcissist so you can be sure to at least keep your guard up if you can't avoid being around them. The benefit is, once you've played the game you know the score and you don't have to play anymore.

Walking on Eggshells

Do you come home and feel like you can never relax? Do you carefully think about what you say so you don't trigger a reaction or argument? Do you dread hearing his car pull into the driveway? You should feel safe in your home. Being on high alert every waking second is depleting your energy.

As she was walking up the stairs to the apartment, Michelle can hear Pink Floyd's The Wall booming. That meant only one thing, Dan was in a bad mood. Michelle needed to make a choice: turn around and come back later or go in and hope she can avoid angering him. She chose to go in. Before she did, she made sure to go over the rules with her daughter. Don't talk to him unless he talks first. Try and eat all your dinner. Don't leave your art supplies out. Don't play your keyboard too loud. Don't play your TV too loud. Don't drink the rest of the milk or tea or Kool aid. Don't leave your socks or shoes in the living room. Those were just the rules for their daughter. Michelle's list was much longer. Don't do the dishes too loudly. Don't leave books on the table. Don't take too long in the shower. And after bedtime, well, just do what he says and wants. It was just easier that way.

No one should live like that. You deserve peace. Your home is your sanctuary. If it isn't, maybe you need to start taking the steps necessary to make your home your castle.

He's the Only One
Your feelings and opinions are rarely validated. He's the only one that matters. He's also the only one allowed to have feelings and opinions. All your feelings do is cause drama for him. Your opinions are wrong if they aren't the same as his. Even if they are the same as his you still can't voice them until after he states his. That way it looks like he's the brains of the operation. You're just there to echo his brilliance.

No Trust
You could be working the night shift at a morgue and he'll still accuse you of cheating on him. Can't account for five dollars out of the bank? You spent it on something and just won't tell him. You must be

doing drugs or you weren't really working; you went to a bar. Like all his behavior this has nothing to do with you. He doesn't trust himself. He knows what goes on in his head and since he is the sun, the moon, and the stars everyone must think like him. That means you. This is a form of projection so you can rest assured knowing that it really is him and not you. The ugly flip side of this coin is you now have some insight into what is going on in his brain. Remember, projection is him focusing on you how he sees himself and his role in the world around him.

Chapter 5

Cut loose

You've had enough. That or he used you up and tossed you out. Either way, you have some work ahead of you now. The biggest thing is not to panic. You can survive this. Your survival rate is 100% so far. You got this.

What not to do

Do not fall for his lies. He has not changed. He will still blame you. The cycle will still continue. He is only coming back because you are his dealer and supply. He can't get his fix anywhere else so, he keeps boomeranging to you. Once he gets what he wants you go right back to square one. All his promises have the sincerity of a disgraced televangelist.

Don't argue. Narcissists thrive on conflict and breed drama. He will start baiting you just for the fun of it. They are button pushers. Save yourself the frustration and do not engage. They will shift blame, throw pity parties, and start singing the poor poor pitiful me blues. He will pick apart your sentences. Think about having your Miranda rights read to you; anything you say or do can and will be held against you. It's all about control. He will do what he deems necessary to control the conversation and win while making you look bad.

Are you a right fighter?

This is an honest question. I've been seeing a lot on here and other social media sites of people that seems to just fight for the sake of fighting. There seems to be no winning because they argue in circles or throw the gauntlet of my way or the highway down. No compromise, no seeing eye to eye. There's not even the old standby of let's agree to disagree. It's seems as if everyone has come down with a case of I'm right-itis with a side of you're wrong-atosis. What happened to civil, healthy debates? What happened to understanding everyone has an opinion and it may not be the same as yours and that's ok? What happened to live and let live? This goes back to my statement of if it doesn't put money in your pocket or take money out then who the hell cares?!

Oh my god! For chuck's sake, people. When did we become so sensitive in our beliefs that when anyone challenges them we call them stupid or worse? All because they don't see things the same way we do? It's not that hard. Just like you want people to listen to you, so do others. Just like you would hate for someone to silence you or treat you as if you don't matter, so does everyone else. Don't be so narcissistic to think you're the only person allowed to have opinions on a subject.

Life is a great big, crazy diamond with a whole bunch of beautiful facets sparkling and shining in the light of the universe. You are one facet in the diamond. Respect your fellow facets. Respect yourself.

Don't beg
After Dan kicked her out, Michelle returned to the house to get the rest of her belongings. Most of them were still packed in boxes so at least that was easier. Dan stood at the top of the stairs while his new girlfriend was sitting in the living room. The stress got a hold of Michelle and she started crying. Crying turned into sobbing. The harsh realization hit her that she had no where to go. With a nine year old daughter to take care of and no clue what she was going to do next, fear set in. She sat at the bottom of those stairs weeping, pleading for him to take her back. Whatever she did wrong, she would fix it. She even went so far to say she didn't care about what happened to their daughter as long as he took her back. That's a phrase he often used against Michelle in so many arguments.

In the end, he did not take her back. The day she thought would be the end of her life, turned out to be a gift. That gift was a bigger and better life. More than she could have ever dreamed for herself and her daughter.

Don't force communication

You can't communicate with a narcopath. Just disengage. You want to remain calm and in control of yourself. He will provoke and prod you. Don't take the bait. Nothing drives a narcopath crazier than when you don't engage with him. His whole goal is for you to start yelling and defending yourself. Then he gets to say he's the victim and you're the aggressor.

Don't go back

Don't take him back or go back to him. Remove the boomerang from your heart. You need to heal. Even though he's done with you he may still try to recruit you to his flying monkey circus for his new target. Don't play his games. Going back to your ex is like drinking milk, finding it's bad, and putting it back hoping it will be better.

Don't apologize

Don't feel sorry for him. That's like saying it was OK for him to do what he did all that time. He robbed you of dreams, goals, and a life.

Every lie and concealment become validated the instant you feel bad for him. No one feels bad for child abusers or wife beaters. Do not feel bad for your abuser. Trust me, he will tell his version of the truth to his friends and family who will give him enough sympathy. It doesn't matter if he's this way due to nature or nurture. He destroys lives and gets off on it.

It won't be easy

    There's a lot to be afraid of. Unfortunately, those things are usually not as bad as we think they are. But we tend to let the fear take us over and hold us down. Could you imagine what your life would be like if you just stopped being afraid? What could you do if you stopped letting the fear rule you? It's ok to have fear. It's ok to be afraid. Just don't let the fear have you. Fear can move you, motivate you, push you. But you have to face it and use it. It won't serve you if you let it keep you locked up on your couch. Trust me, I know because that's what I've let it do to me. I have given my fears permission to tell me what I can do and what I can't. So I'm giving it up. I'm giving up my fear. I'm rising above it and I'm ready to see what I can do. Are you ready to give up your fear? Are you ready to see what you can do and where you will go?

    The first step is acceptance. Accept he didn't love you. You are lovable. You are worthy of love. He wasn't capable of loving you. Love is unconditional. But he put so many limitations on it that no one could live up to those standards. His whole basis for love is his own selfish expectations and entitlement. Once you can accept that then you can start healing.

Leaving it in the past is the second step even if you get kicked out. Moving on is hard, especially if leaving wasn't your choice. Understand that before he discarded you he was already working on his next victim. By the time he gets rid of you he already has your replacement. And he will take great pleasure showing her off in front of you. See her as what she is, his next piece of human wreckage, another trophy for his wall, You will never get an apology. There will most likely be no closure. All the work of picking up and gluing the pieces back together is all on you.

Friends and family may not be supportive. They won't understand. That's OK. They were fooled by the illusion too. They have a decision to make, believe you or him. Don't be surprised at the people who stick by him and think you're evil incarnate. He didn't just play his games with you.

Michelle had a tight group of friends when she lived in the Northeast. When she started dating Dan her friends slowly stopped interacting with her as much. By the time she moved to the Midwest with him she may have seen her friends once a month. As the years went by there were Facebook chats and text messages but they weren't the same level of friendship as they used to be. Something had changed. Something was missing. Her friends loved Michelle, however they hated Dan. They hated what he had done to her. It was months after the relationship ended that Michelle's friend, Baja, told her they had all secretly been happy Dan was out of the picture. Michelle said she was, too.

Chapter 6

Healing

Why me?

It's not you, it's him. He's angry he's weak and powerless. He may have been born with a sense of entitlement or he may have developed it later in life. Either way, his expectations are unreasonable. You owe him. Everyone owes him. If you give him an ounce he takes a pound and wants ten more. You were supposed to ignore everyone and everything for his happiness. That includes your kids and yourself. But remember, his expectations are so high that nothing you do will be good enough. Ever. Nothing you give will be enough. He is a black hole sucking in all light and life destroying it in its gravitational field.

Fix it. Fix it. Fix it.

You may be a fixer. Fixers find people to fix. Fixers clean up the mess caused by the narcissist. They will also make excuses for narc's bad behavior. Narcs feed off fixers' need for approval. Fixers are a type of empath.

Empaths feel others pain. If you're an empath you may be able to read people. The news bothers you more than the average person. Bright lights and loud sounds hurt. Violence makes you physically ill. Some peoples' vibrations make you nervous and shaky. You can feel others' emotional states. You know dead on when someone is lying to you. Sad stories or movies are too much for you. You have a hard time saying no to people. You attract broken people. You have a need to fix everything and everyone to make the world (or at least your corner of it) better.

Guilt trip for free

You weren't involved. You had no control. However, you feel you should have known a bad situation was going to happen and you didn't so now you feel guilty. I sometimes joke about living in an Italian Irish Catholic family and that's why I have this guilt. This guilt is one of the reasons your narc targeted you. Think about it. How much easier is it to blame someone for all the wrongs in the world than someone who already feels guilty.

Lonely in a crowded room

Because of your sensitivity you feel misunderstood and alone. Even though you have close friends, they still don't quite get that you'd rather be home listening to Billie Holliday, drinking hot chocolate instead of standing in the loud, smoky, crowded bar that's draining your energy like an oil well in Texas. The narc senses your solitude and plays on that. He tells you he's also a lonely spirit who has never understood by others.

He makes you think you're the same. Nothing could be farther from the truth. He will use your feelings of being an outcast to pull you away from friends and family and isolate you.

I left now what

Congrats on getting away. Now watch out for the smear campaign and the poor, poor, pitiful me routine. He's going to act as if you're the one that hurt him. Remember, he's the victim. This is when you find out who's with you and who's just a flying monkey. You're going to want to vent and defend yourself against these attacks to anyone who will listen. Unfortunately, not every shoulder to cry on is helpful. Some come with wings to carry them back and tell the narc everything you've said. This just fuels the victim image he's trying to uphold. Don't add gas to the bonfire. If you need to let off steam, I suggest a journal or the app Whisper. Whisper is anonymous making it pretty safe to cry about the unfairness of your situation. For the record, it is unfair. You are totally justified in your feelings. Bottling them up isn't going to help. Just be mindful of who offers their ears to you.

No contact or limited contact.

So much effort and time and energy has been put into making you think you can't survive on your own. No contact gives you time and space to heal. That means no texts, phone calls, emails, or Facebook messages. In fact, go ahead and unfriend, delete, and block him and his flying monkey circus. You don't need spies running and tattling on you every time you post something. And he will try to contact you, either directly or through his flying monkeys. Despite what he told you repeatedly he needs you more than you need him.

Don't listen to the candy coated poison. He will make negotiations and promises. "I'll change. I'll be better. Just come back. Baby, I love you." No. He doesn't. He won't change. He never loved you. He loved the idea of love. The newness, the hope, the potential, the fairy tale. All which he will never have because all he knows how to do is use, devalue, and discard.

Cut him out like the malignant tumor he is. No one thinks, "Gee, I miss that cancerous tumor and the way it was choking the life out of me. Maybe I should check in on it and see how it's doing." No one thinks, "That tumor pissed me off. Even though its been 6 months since I had it cut out, I'm going to call it and tell it how I feel." No. No one thinks any of that. Your ex is a tumor.

You have strength in your feet to get back on them. Don't use that strength running back to the abuser that stole that strength from you to start with. For now you need to heal.

It is hard if you have kids together. There may be visitation orders that allow him contact with the kids. I suggest asking friends or family to do the operation kid swap for a little bit. After a while you'll be able to start going with your proxy and eventually by yourself. You will not be able to control what your kids hear from your ex. You can only control what they hear from you. Don't talk negatively about your ex in front of the kids. It's going to suck when they tell you all the fun and interesting things your ex narc is saying about you. Don't respond. Don't retaliate. It is a good idea to look into counseling for your kids. Their world is turning upside down. Depending on their ages, may not quite understand what's going on.

Share your story.

It will be scary. You'll worry what others will say or think. And some will say you're lying. You're not sharing your story for them you're doing it for you. You're doing it for everyone in a relationship with a narcissistic psychopath. "You own everything that happened to you. Tell your stories. If people wanted you to write warmly about them, they should've behaved better." Anne Lamott

Create boundaries

You need to build walls. You need hard, firm rules about what you will allow in your life. You get to do that now. It's your life. Say no without guilt. Say yes because you want to, not because you feel like you have to. Your happiness is your responsibility. You are not responsible for anyone else's happiness.

Its OK to grieve

Grieve for who you believed he was. Grieve for the false image you fell in love with. Grieve for who you were before all this. Grieve for that part of you he stole. Grieve for friends you lost. Grieve for memories that are lies and memories you can't remember.

Chapter 7
You are a survivor

Reclaiming yourself

I'm lying here, next to my sleeping toddler son, and something occurs to me. I am not the same person I was 3 years ago. Quite frankly, I'm not the same person I was 3 weeks ago. And I hope I'm not the same person next year or even next month. What's changed, you might ask. Simple. I have.

A few years back, I had a conversation with my brother. Now you need to understand my brother is not a hold back kind of guy. When I was pregnant with my daughter and visiting home, he was informing me that if my child were ugly he would let me know. As we're talking a girl walked by with a baby. And as they walked by his says, "Like that. That's an ugly baby. If your baby looks like that I'll tell you you have an ugly baby." He's not rude. He just doesn't see the purpose of the formality of politeness and political correctness. So, here we are talking and he tells me he misses me. "I miss you, too," I say. He says, "No, not your physical body or presence. I miss who you used to be. I miss miss Tigger. I miss my Tigger." I knew immediately what he meant.

See, I used to be the hyper one, the excited one, the funny, goofy, silly, random one. Hence my nickname, Tigger. I guess somewhere along the way I allowed people and situations to steal parts of me, parts of my soul. It's hard to be bouncy, flouncy, pouncy, trouncy when you're told how embarrassing you are and that you need to grow up. They say sticks and stones will break your bones, but words will never hurt me. That's nothing but lies. Words hurt. Words from others become our inner monologue. So over the years more and more of my true self I gave away.

Yes, I said given away. I gave permission to those people, events, and situations to defeat me. I allowed it to happen. I was full well aware of what was happening and I let it keep going.

Well, at least until 4 years ago. Through a series of events, both fortunate and un, I started to reclaim parts of my soul. Bit by bit I've started to find relics and artifacts of the old me. Through a lot of work, love, and forgiveness, I glued those pieces back together.

One of my favorite stories is how the Japanese would repair pottery with gold to fill in the cracks. Just because something is broken doesn't make it ugly. The gold shows that the cracks helped make it more beautiful. Now that pottery had a story to tell. Now it had a history.

I'd like to think of myself like those pots. I used to think of myself as damaged. Useless and broken, afraid to talk or even be around people. But it's my cracks that have made me stronger, better, and able to tell my story. Now I can help others who are also losing themselves and finding themselves.

I'll always remember when my mom saw me at Disney World after my breakup. She said, "I found my best friend again."

So did I, Ma, so did I.

You're worth it

Ok, my lovies, I'm about to lay some truth on you.

You are amazing. That's right. You read that correctly. You are an amazing, brilliant creation. Whether you believe we are a product of a deity, or the universe, or evolution, or aliens it doesn't change the fact that you are incredible. You are made of the same things that make stars and kitties and coffee, ooh coffee.

You are capable of wonderful feats of humanity. You have the power to make someone smile, laugh, and in general feel good. You could be the motivating force that causes someone to research and discover cures for deadly diseases. You could be the inspiration for a piece of art that will fascinate people for generations. You could be the driving force behind an award winning Broadway show.

The point is, you are so much more than bills, and working just to get by. You are a passionate, loving, living, breathing human. And you are surrounded by people who need you, your energy, your creativity, your fire. There is something about you that someone needs. It may be a song, or poem, or just the fact that you are there to listen when they need it most.

You matter. Your life matters. Your voice matters. Your presence matters. You make a difference in this world just by being here. Thank you for coming through. Thank you for being you. If no one has said it to you, I am proud of you. I am grateful for you. And I love you.

how i decided to live my dreams

If we have learned one thing this year I would say that the lesson is no one is guaranteed a tomorrow. We have seen shocking celebrity deaths and unspeakable mass murders. All these people taken before we were ready for them to go. Most likely before they were ready as well.

Thinking about it all I found myself wondering what dreams were left unfulfilled. What goals will never be reached? How many stories will never be told? Poems unwritten? Movies never produced? Songs never sung? How many people have passed this year alone that never lived to their full potential?

I realized the other day that I am at a strange and scary age. I'm coming to an age where the days behind me outnumber the ones ahead. My parents are the same age my father in law was when he passed. My heroes are all leaving us to join the other stars in the sky. It all got me wondering what I'm leaving. Not just for my kids, but for everyone. What would my legacy be? What was I leaving behind? Why wasn't I living my dream?

There was only one answer. What was I leaving? Two kids that I hopefully raised into decent human beings. Then the real question hit me. What was I living? Was I playing it safe? Was I just letting the world pass me by as I sat hoping I made a difference? Was I using the gifts I was given by the universe? Why wasn't I living to my potential? Why wasn't I doing what I've always wanted to do?

Fear and laziness. It was that simple. I had to take responsibility for my lack of passion. I was lazy. It's hard work finding out how to do things you don't know how. What's an SEO? Adwords? Monetize? Nah. I just wanted to write. How do I boost my audience? Wait, people are going to read this? No. I can't handle that. Too many opinions, too much rejection. Only in your dreams would someone want to read what you write. No, I'll just stick to my hand written journals. But I'm tired and I don't have time. I've only been on Pinterest five times today. And posted on Facebook ten times. I just don't have time to write.

What changed? I couldn't keep avoiding the fact that I had something to say. I had something to share and something I wanted to leave to the world. I wanted to leave my sense of humor, positivity, and words so others could read them. I wanted people laugh, learn, and feel they are not the only ones going through difficult times. Whatever it may be you are not the only one.

I didn't want to be on my death bed and look up only to see my dreams in front of me. I didn't want to hear them say, "Only you could have given us life. Only you could have given us a voice. All these words now will go unsaid because you didn't tell them. And now we will die with you. Why didn't you follow your dream?"

I couldn't handle that. And even though it is a daily battle with fear, and motivation, and a toddler who thinks he needs to be on my lap while I'm writing I still do it. I live my dream every day. Some days I write better than others. I'm still working on proofreading. Sorry, mom.

Do not leave your dreams in your head. Live your dreams. Each and every day. Leave them here for us. Your dreams and your passion and your work could be the inspiration for so many others. It may even be your words that get turned into dream quotes and motivation memes on Facebook. It will be hard, and you'll get discouraged and distracted, but it will be worth it.

You have an amazing beautiful future ahead of you. That chapter of your story is over. Turn the page and keep writing. The best is yet to come. And as always, you're worth it. I'm grateful for you. I'm proud of you. And I love you. Now go out there and be strong, beautiful, loving survivors.

Made in the USA
Middletown, DE
27 August 2018